Original title:
Sap and Sentiment

Copyright © 2025 Creative Arts Management OÜ
All rights reserved.

Author: Simon Fairchild
ISBN HARDBACK: 978-1-80567-235-7
ISBN PAPERBACK: 978-1-80567-534-1

Fragrant Offers

In a garden of giggles, the flowers plot,
They whisper sweet secrets and love that's hot.
A daisy proposes, a rose winks back,
Yet all turn their heads when the tulip cracks.

Bees buzz with laughter, on nectar they feast,
While butterflies dance, an extravagant beast.
They trade silly puns in the soft morning light,
Nature's own humor, a whimsical sight.

Essence Encased

In a jar of delight, pickles all lined,
There's joy in each crunch, a pickle-eyed bind.
A dill so enamored, hooked on its brine,
Says, "Life's just a snack; look at me shine!"

Garlic whispers secrets to cucumbers ripe,
In a tangy embrace, they giggle and type.
They toast with each crunch, a refreshingly fun,
Bottled up laughter, when dinner's begun.

Beneath the Bark

Underneath the surface, the trees share tales,
Of squirrels in tuxedos and acorned gales.
They giggle at winds that tickle their leaves,
While raccoons tell stories, in pranks they believe.

A woodpecker's knock is a rhythmic surprise,
While beetles do tap dance, to the laughter that flies.
Roots deep in the soil, they chuckle and sway,
Woodland humor thriving, in their own funny way.

The Tears of Timber

Oh, the wood's gone weepy, sap sliding like tears,
Caught in a giggle, it calms all its fears.
'Twas a joke on the bark, said the maple to pine,
"Your needles are sharp, but my heart's feeling fine!"

With a tickle of breeze, the branches all quake,
Crying out giggles with every small shake.
The logs in the pile groan with laughter and grins,
From the folds of old forest, where all the fun begins.

Essence of the Evergreen

In the forest, a tree took a sip,
Whispered secrets through foliage's grip.
Bark stayed snug in its woody wear,
Giggling in sunlight, without a care.

Squirrels joked with acorns in hand,
Dancing around, making a band.
Pine cones snickered, dropped with a thud,
While laughter echoed, rolling like buds.

Heartstrings and Harvests

Pumpkins grinned in the patch so bright,
Chasing away all the chill of the night.
Tomatoes blushed in the warm sunshine,
Sharing their sauce in a quirky design.

Corn giggled as it swayed in the breeze,
Tickling the cobs, such playful tease!
Each bite a chuckle, each crunch a cheer,
Harvest's playground, the end of the year.

Veiled Emotions in Amber

A jar of honey sat snug on the shelf,
Dreaming of flowers, lost in itself.
Buzzing bees winked with sticky embrace,
Tickling the senses with sweet, silly grace.

Candles flickered with teasing glows,
Wax dripped like jokes that nobody knows.
Singing of laughs in a din of delight,
Eagerly waiting for the upside of night.

The Sweetness of Seasons

Spring tickled the ground, ready to play,
With puddle jumps keeping grey skies at bay.
While flowers winked, waved their bright hues,
Played hopscotch right on the morning dew.

Summer sang loud with a bubblegum voice,
Ice cream cones made the kids rejoice.
Laughter erupted in warm golden rays,
Sticky fingers clutching sweet, sunny days.

Harvest Moon Heartstrings

Under the moonlit skies we dance,
With pies and giggles in a trance.
The pumpkins laugh, they roll away,
Wishing us a happy day!

We juggle apples, slip and slide,
With silly hats, we take our pride.
While squirrels plot their nutty schemes,
We chase the shadows of our dreams.

Circles of Healing

In a circle we all gather tight,
With rubber chickens, laughter's light.
A yoga pose turned into a flop,
The laughter echoes, none can stop!

The quirkiest souls find their grace,
As we twist and turn, oh what a race!
With yoga mats and funny pants,
We spin the fables of our chance.

Tributes and Treetops

Up in the treetops, we do sway,
Waving to birds that chirp and play.
We build our forts with sticks and leaves,
And send them flying with gentle heaves.

A paper crown we craft with glee,
Declared as king, who'll disagree?
The squirrels giggle, they join the fun,
In royal antics, there's laughter spun.

The Glow of Garnered Innocence

With jars of fireflies, we catch the spark,
Bright as our giggles in the dark.
A game of tag beneath the stars,
Chasing wishes from old tin jars.

Our innocence a wild delight,
In laughter shared, we take our flight.
With whispered secrets, we glow so bright,
In a world of wonder, pure and light.

Veins of the Soul

In a tree's pulse, a giggle flows,
Nature's secret, only she knows.
A squirrel wiggles, in joyful spree,
Chasing shadows, so carefree.

Branches creak with laughter, bright,
Every rustle feels just right.
Leaves dance, twirling to and fro,
While the world spins with a glow.

Bark whispers tales of playful din,
A forest party about to begin.
With each breeze, secrets spill,
Nature chuckles, hearty and shrill.

A Lattice of Love

In my garden, a tangled vine,
Entwined hearts, looking divine.
A bumblebee buzzing, feeling grand,
Sweet serenades in this land.

Petals flit like butterflies,
Whispers share the silly ties.
With every bloom, a chuckle grows,
As nature paints with vibrant shows.

Insects play, a comical crew,
Tickling flowers in morning dew.
A daisy winks, a tulip sighs,
As giggles echo through the skies.

Reflections in Amber

Sunlight spills like syrup bright,
On amber dreams taking flight.
A ladybug dons a polka dot gown,
On a leaf throne, wearing a crown.

Time ticks funny in this sphere,
Where wishes dance and disappear.
Honeyed laughter fills the air,
As memories swirl without a care.

In the pond, frogs sing their song,
Croaking laughter, all day long.
Ripples ripple with sweet delight,
As nature joins in their playful fight.

The Nectar of Longing

A tiny bee with big dreams,
Buzzing 'round like it redeems.
It flits from flower to flower bold,
In search of sweetness, stories unfold.

Velvet petals wink at the sky,
While the sun rolls around to say hi.
Bumblebees bumble, a comical chase,
As nectar dreams sweetly embrace.

Each drop tasted, a giggle shared,
In a world where nobody's scared.
With each sip, a joke is spun,
In this dance, we all have fun.

Nature's Embrace

In the garden, a squirrel took flight,
Chasing its tail, what a silly sight!
Flowers giggle as the breeze teases,
As bees waltz round, oh how it pleases!

The sun sneezes, the clouds all chuckle,
While daisies dance without a struggle.
A worm wiggles, saying 'Look at me!'
The laughter echoes among the trees.

Butterflies dressed in polka dot cheer,
Whisper secrets that only they hear.
Rabbits hop in a lively parade,
While nature's mischief is artfully played.

The leaves rustle with a playful rhyme,
As nature spins tales of silly time.
With every rustle and giggling sound,
Life's playful spirit is truly found.

The Soul's Brew

Pour the moonlight, add some glee,
Stirred with giggles, just wait and see!
A sprinkle of joy from the morning dew,
Makes every soul pop, just like new.

The stars gossip, can you hear their tales?
Over steaming cups, their laughter sails.
A dash of whimsy, a pinch of fun,
This brew is ready, it's second to none!

Laughter bubbles like a bright potion,
While clouds parade in merry motion.
Each sip brings smiles, oh what a treat,
Join in the laughter, life's rhythm is sweet.

Hold up your cups to the sparkling night,
Joy is the spark, it's pure delight.
With every cheer and every toast,
Let's celebrate what we love the most.

Infused with Love

Gather round, let's share a laugh,
Mix in some giggles by the glass half.
Berries are blushing, all ripe and round,
With every taste, pure joy is found.

Honey drips, like a sticky hug,
Each drop a giggle, snug as a bug.
Stir in some sunshine, warm and bright,
This potion's ready, now feels just right.

Candied laughter rolls on our tongues,
While harmony's played on laughter's drums.
A swirl of kindness, it's plain to see,
Infused with warmth, as love should be.

Raise your glass and let's toast high,
With silly stories that never die.
For every moment wrapped in cheer,
With hearts so light, let's hold them dear.

Embracing the Elements

The sun chuckles as it peeks through,
Tickling the leaves with a bright hello.
Clouds play dress-up, fluffy and wide,
As nature's circus joins the ride.

Rain drops dance with a pitter pat,
While muddy puddles invite a splat!
Wind whistles tunes that make trees sway,
Together they frolic, come join the play!

Lightning bugs spark with a wink and a grin,
Drawing doodles in the air, let's begin!
Each splash, each twirl, is a joyful dance,
In nature's arms, we take a chance.

Embrace the world with a hearty cheer,
Nature's in stitches, let's spread the gear!
With every giggle, the earth spins fast,
In this happy chaos, let's hold steadfast.

Euphoria in Viscosity

A sticky joke upon my shoe,
Laughter glues me, what to do?
Life's syrup drips, it coats the day,
Making smiles in a gooey way.

Friends think I'm just a walking mess,
With every step, I must confess.
A sugar rush that makes me dance,
In this sweet slip, I find my chance.

Beneath the trees, we glide and slip,
Like kids again on a candy trip.
Laughter echoes through the grove,
In this charm, we feel the love.

Embracing the Sweetness

A splash of honey on my toast,
I giggle loud, it's what I love most.
Every drizzle tells a tale,
Of tasty joys that never fail.

I plan to swim in chocolate lakes,
While dodging every nutty shake.
With frosty sprinkles on my head,
Laughter lingers, joy widespread.

Sticky fingers, what a sight,
Sweets by day, dreams by night.
Life's a buffet, let's seize the fun,
In every bite, we come undone.

A Woodland Reverie

In the woods, where squirrels play,
They chase the bees, and hug the hay.
Mushrooms giggle near the trees,
While branches sway in every breeze.

The ants hold dances on the ground,
With tiny steps, they twirl around.
Frolicsome roots beneath my feet,
Each step is a chuckle, oh so sweet!

Bubbles float from bubbling brooks,
Nature's humor in all its nooks.
In this realm, we laugh away,
A leafy party, come what may.

Resonance of the Heart

In a rhythm, my heart sings loud,
Frogs and crickets join the crowd.
With each thump a giggle flows,
As I dance with my silly woes.

Tickled by the autumn leaves,
Every step, my spirit weaves.
Laughter echoes in the park,
Joyful shades from dawn till dark.

A flutter in my chest so bright,
Like fireflies that light the night.
In this jive, let's play our part,
With every laugh, we find the heart.

Amber Veins

In the forest, trees do sway,
Their giggles echo, come what may.
Bees in top hats, quite a sight,
Buzzing dances in the light.

Sap drips down, a sticky flow,
Like sweetened jokes, they steal the show.
Laughter bubbles, oh so bright,
Woodland critters take their flight.

Squirrels barter with a grin,
Trading acorns, let the fun begin!
A riddle wrapped in bark and bark,
Where laughter finds its cozy spark.

So let us join this woodland spree,
Drink from the cup of joy and glee.
Amber veins, life's jestful art,
Nature's humor, heart to heart.

Whispers of the Heartwood

The whispering branches share their tales,
Of rooster parades and hedgehog trails.
Frogs tell jokes in a leap and bound,
While trees chuckle with leaves around.

In heartwood creeks, the laughter flows,
Mice in bowties, striking a pose.
Elk in slippers tap their toes,
Where humor spreads like summer's rose.

Stone-faced owls with eyes so round,
Chiming in with a goofy sound.
In this forest, pranks take flight,
As creatures giggle 'til the night.

So gather 'round, let joy ignite,
In whispers soft, it's pure delight.
With every chuckle, life ascends,
In heartwood's humor, joy transcends.

The Nectar of Nostalgia

Collecting memories, sticky and sweet,
Like honeyed dreams, a tasty treat.
The ants wear glasses, reading the news,
While old bees tell tales of daring snooze.

Each drop of reminiscence brings a grin,
Recalling games of hide and kin.
A squirrel's dance from branch to branch,
Makes all the woodland creatures prance.

Fungi giggle under moonlit skies,
Swapping stories, oh what a surprise!
A time machine forged in tree sap,
With every laughter finds a gap.

Sprinkling sweetness on every age,
Nostalgia's nectar fills the stage.
So take a sip and chuckle here,
Where past and joy are always near.

Liquid Memories

In bubbling brooks, the past unfolds,
Liquid tales that time beholds.
A fish in a bowler, quite absurd,
With whiskers dancing, oh what a word!

Trees swim in giggles, splashing cheer,
Where frogs serenade with froggy flair.
Nostalgic ripples, a playful breeze,
Transport us back with such sweet ease.

Old jars of laughter line the shore,
Each one bursting with tales of yore.
Sipping puddles, we find the jest,
In liquid memories, laughter's quest.

So gather 'round this merry stream,
Where fun flows freely, like a dream.
Drop your worries, take a dip,
In joyous waters, let laughter rip!

Tears of the Earth

When rivers cry, they make a splash,
A giggle from the hills, a bubbly clash.
Mountains chuckle as they shed their tears,
Nature's laughter ringing in our ears.

Clouds puff up, full of jokes and jests,
Rolling across the sky, wearing vests.
They tickle the trees, which start to dance,
In a silly waltz, they take a chance.

Mud pies launch from playful streams,
As frogs leap high, living their dreams.
The sun beams down with a toothy grin,
While flowers sway, joining in this spin.

Sometimes we trip on a puddle's prank,
Splashing around, we forget to thank.
So here's to the earth and its funny ways,
In every drop, there's joy that stays.

Viscous Memories

In a jar full of goo, we find our past,
Sticky tales of joy that hold steadfast.
A gooey giggle, a translucent grin,
Each wiggle and wobble, new stories begin.

The syrupy echoes of laughter float,
As time slides by in a sweetened boat.
With every glimmer, a chuckle appears,
Thickened memories chased away fears.

A puddle of thought, all jumbled and warm,
We stir up emotions, a playful swarm.
Honey drips down with whispers of fun,
Creating a chaos once the day's done.

So slather on laughter, spread it around,
With each sticky drop, new joys abound.
In findings and frolics, we're never alone,
For every sweet moment is a memory grown.

Liquid Emotions

In a bottle of joy, we twist and shake,
Bubbles of laughter when it's at stake.
A splash of delight, a wave of cheer,
Flowing like rivers that tickle the ear.

Beneath the surface, feelings swirl,
Each droplet dances, giving a twirl.
With every giggle, the colors collide,
Creating a rainbow that can't be denied.

Pour out the happiness, let it stream,
A cascade of chuckles, a whimsical dream.
Sprinkled with humor, like dew on grass,
A drink of pure fun, let's raise a glass!

So as we bask in this juicy delight,
We'll sip on laughter, morning to night.
For in each liquid, emotions engage,
Creating a wacky, unforgettable stage.

Glimmers of Essence

In a pond of giggles, the essence gleams,
Reflections of joy in the sunbeam dreams.
Little fish wink, with a splashy tease,
As frogs croak jokes to draw out the leaves.

Sparkles of laughter twinkle above,
A cheerful breeze, like a playful shove.
The stars giggle softly, the moon gives a wink,
While shadows break out, in mischief they sink.

Petals are blushing, embracing the fun,
Dancing to tunes that the crickets have spun.
With a jolly breeze and a warm sunny face,
Nature's a party, a joyous embrace.

So gather together, let moments uplift,
In glimmers of essence, we find our gift.
For every shimmer has stories to share,
A whimsical journey that floats in the air.

Beneath the Canopy

Under leafy arches, critters prance,
Squirrels plot their nutty romance.
Rain drops fall with a tiny twinge,
Hoping to cause a little cringe.

Budging blooms in the gentle breeze,
Whisper secrets that make us sneeze.
Bees bumble in their drunken dance,
Nature's humor in a fleeting glance.

Lizards bask, with tails that sway,
In the sun's warm and playful play.
A frog croaks a tune, quite absurd,
Leave the bad vibes, let laughter be heard.

Under the canopy, we all unite,
Sharing giggles till the day turns night.
With the critters and plants all around,
Joyful chaos is nature's sound.

Sweet and Subtle

Beneath the boughs where shadows dare,
The flowers chuckle without a care.
Petals flirt in colors bright,
Pulling faces at the firefly flight.

Honey drips with a sticky glee,
While ants march home, a sight to see.
Windows open for the sun's warm hugs,
Nature's jokes are like tired pugs.

A breeze rolls in with a cheeky shove,
Tickling noses, it's a push and shove.
Laughter echoes through the leafy maze,
In this sweet world where happiness plays.

So grab your friends and wander wide,
Join Mother Nature on this ride.
In every corner, a chuckle awaits,
Sometimes even love is what it states.

Nature's Heartstrings

On the branch, a bird starts singing,
While a rabbit's ear is blissfully flinging.
With a hop, it snickers at the cat,
A hunter confused by a nimble spat.

The flowers giggle when the wind blows,
Petals tickling each other's toes.
A sunflower winks with golden pride,
At bees that bump and buzz, side by side.

The clouds roll in, wearing a frown,
As raindrops start to tumble down.
But puddles form for splashes of fun,
Joy and laughter under the sun!

Nature weaves a tapestry bright,
In every rustle, a playful bite.
With laughter echoing like bright chimes,
Life is a joke that unfolds in rhymes.

Tendrils of Thought

In the garden, a vine starts to flirt,
With the fence post wearing dirt like a skirt.
Buds poke out, curious and spry,
Wondering just how high they can fly.

The soil chuckles, a warm embrace,
Giving sprouts a delightful place.
Worms wiggle through with a cheeky grin,
In their underground party, let's all join in!

Ladybugs parade with tiny spots,
Flicking off dew in playful knots.
The sunbeams laugh as shadows bend,
As nature chills out, around the bend.

So pluck your worries from the vine,
Dance in the breeze, let your heart incline.
For in this world of green and cheer,
Silly moments bring us near.

The Reservoir of Dreams

In a jar on the shelf, a wish so bright,
Hops around like a playful kite.
It spills over cookies, it giggles a tune,
As it dreams of being a big balloon.

A squirrel in a coat, quite dapper and grand,
Dances with acorns, in a shuffling band.
It steals all the snacks, then gives a quick wink,
And leaves trails of laughter, who'd ever think?

By the pond, the frogs sing silly croons,
In bow ties made of paper and balloons.
They leap with a jig, and hop with flair,
With dreams of a world, where frogs can share.

Jars filled with giggles, and wishes on crack,
With bubbles and smiles, we'll never look back!
Let's toast to the dreams, the fun they bring,
In a world of wonders, we'll always sing!

Whispers of Affection

A squeeze of a lemon, with sugar on top,
Two spoons and a kiss, in a green polka dot.
Whispers collide like bubbles in tea,
Floating around, just like you and me.

An owl in glasses, quite wise and astute,
Reads the fine print in a fruit loop suit.
It nods in agreement, sips sweet charade,
In a world where bananas just dance and parade.

Two ants hold hands, what a funny sight,
Discussing their plans for a sweet candlelight.
With crumbs as their dinner, they raise little cheers,
While butterflies chuckle, hiding their tears.

So busy we get with our odd little quirks,
With laughter and joy that still strangely works.
Found in the moments, we'll always connect,
Like taffy and laughter, sweet and perfect!

Melodies in the Canopy

A parrot in rhythm, with feathers of jade,
Sings to the branches that softly cascade.
It tickles the leaves with a feathered song,
As squirrels jump in, showing who's right and wrong.

The whispers of branches, they giggle and sway,
Making the clouds come out to play.
With sunbeams of laughter, they pirouette bright,
Spreading their joy in the shimmering light.

A hedgehog on drums, with sticks made of grass,
Taps out a beat, that's sure to surpass.
The raccoons join in, with a bandana flair,
Rocking the night with their wild, furry hair.

So dance with the leaves, let melodies bloom,
In a forest where giggles dispel all the gloom.
With each little note, we'll float in a dream,
Where laughter is king, and silliness beams!

Threads of the Heart

With a needle and thread, tales weave a dance,
Stitching together a whimsical chance.
A patchwork of giggles and whims by the yard,
Creating a quilt that's lovingly starred.

In the attic, a sock claims it's royalty,
Discussing its kingdom with utmost loyalty.
Each thread sings of adventures and glee,
While buttons roll 'round for some tea and spree.

A spider spins jokes in a silky cocoon,
Weaving together a bright, funny tune.
While moths in tuxedos flap about,
Chasing the dreams they can't live without.

Through stitches and laughter, we mend and create,
For hearts that connect, they can never curtail.
With each little thread, we'll craft a new start,
In a fabric of joy that warms every heart!

Memorable Melodies of Maple

In the trees, a syrup trick,
Honey drips, isn't that slick?
Bears dance under the sweet sun,
While raccoons plot just for fun.

Silly songs the squirrels sing,
To the beat of the maple swing.
Sticky paws and smiles wide,
Nature's joy — let's take a ride!

The leaves giggle in the breeze,
As critters play with silly ease.
Laughter echoes through the woods,
While nature dances, oh so good!

With every drop, a chuckle found,
In the sweetness all around.
Maple melodies fill the air,
A funny tale, beyond compare!

Tapping into Time

Once upon a tapping spree,
Woodpeckers knocking with such glee.
In their rhythm, giggles bloom,
Whispers of the forest loom.

A sly old fox joins the scene,
Dancing like a wobbly machine.
Every beat a tale untold,
Of sticky dreams and hearts of gold.

The maple trees clap their hands,
Underneath the sunlit bands.
Rabbits leap with joyous zest,
In this oddball, humorous fest.

Time flows like syrup, oh so sweet,
In this world where critters meet.
Funny moments carved in bark,
As laughter echoes after dark!

Gold and Grit

In the forest, treasures shine,
A golden drop, oh so divine!
But the ants march with a frown,
Calculated moves, in their gown.

Winking at a clumsy bear,
Who stumbled on a branch with flair.
With grit and gumption, he stood tall,
Just to watch a squirrel fall!

Maples glow in the sunset glow,
Casting shadows on the show.
Laughter spills like maple brew,
In this place of silly view.

All life's battles, sweet and rough,
Unfold with humor, never tough.
Gilded dreams, with a twist of fun,
Crafted where the wild things run!

Ebb and Flow of Affection

A river runs, so wild and free,
Where fish flirt while sipping tea.
Splashing jokes under the moon,
Their scales spark laughter - such a boon!

The turtles race to catch a ride,
With friendly banter, full of pride.
As every wave brings in a jest,
Nature's rhythm, truly blessed.

Old logs drift, with tales to tell,
Of lovesick crickets, ringing a bell.
In this tide of funny sight,
Heartfelt chuckles fill the night.

As currents twist and moments flow,
A dance of warmth, to and fro.
In these waters, joy does blend,
A laughter line that has no end!

Nature's Emotive Touch

In the garden where giggles grow,
Bees buzz gossip, and flowers bestow.
Trees whisper secrets, such wild chatter,
While squirrels plot laughs and playful banter.

Frogs croak jokes in the calming pond,
The sun grins down, ensuring we're fond.
Clouds roll by with a soft, puffy smile,
Nature's antics, oh, they stretch for miles!

Butterflies dance in a colorful spree,
Rustling leaves play secrets for free.
Nature knows that humor's entwined,
With chuckles and smiles, we're joyfully bind.

So let's join in nature's wild play,
Where the funny side rules the day.
Watch for the blossoms, pure delight,
In the symphony of joy, everything's bright!

Currents of Connection

Waves of laughter crash on the shore,
Crabs tell jokes, then scurry for more.
Seagulls squawk with comical grace,
Nature's humor, an endless embrace.

Rivers giggle as they twist and twine,
Flowing with joy, a rhythmic design.
Fish pop up, sharing tales of the day,
In this watery world, they laugh and play.

Rainbows arching bring colors so bright,
Each hue chuckles under sunlight.
Weather systems tease with playful flair,
Clouds tickle the sky, oh, what a pair!

So dive into joy, let currents sweep,
In the flow of laughter, secrets keep.
With every splash, giggles arise,
In nature's connection, let our hearts rise!

Physiological Affection

The heart skips beats with a fluttering cheer,
While ticklish moments draw the loved ones near.
A nudge, a poke, the giggles appearing,
In this dance of nerves, joy is endearing.

Hugs burst forth with snugged affection,
Laughter sends waves of happy reflection.
Noses crinkle at jokes so absurd,
And every smile's louder than a bird.

Knees buckle in laughter, a sight so sweet,
As bodies sway, feeling the beat.
Every chuckle, a tickle that soars,
In this wild rhythm, love's never a chore.

So let's bounce and jive, let spirits collide,
With each burst of joy, let laughter reside.
In this dance of life, we sway and share,
With funny connections, our hearts laid bare!

Twilight's Caress

As twilight falls, shadows start to play,
Fireflies blink, in a whimsical ballet.
The moon chuckles softly, a gentle glow,
Whispering jokes only night critters know.

Crickets chirp sonnets in rhythmic delight,
While owls crack wise from their perch in the night.
The breeze teases leaves, a soft, silly kiss,
Nature's laughter, a moment of bliss.

Stars giggle twinkling in celestial glee,
Their shimmer creates cosmic jubilee.
Each glowing orb, a joke in the air,
Twilight's embrace, oh, beyond compare!

So let us bask in this cheeky scene,
Where laughter weaves through the in-between.
In twilight's caress, we're all invited,
In the magic of night, laughter ignited!

Golden Threads of Emotion

In the garden of giggles, I see,
A vine swings a joke, wild and free.
Leaves whisper secrets, oh so bright,
While flowers exchange tales in delight.

A bumblebee chuckles, buzzing around,
Telling the daisies, "You're quite renowned!"
Laughter spills over with every breeze,
Tickling the branches, oh what a tease!

In this canopy of chuckles and cheer,
Even the mushrooms are grinning ear to ear.
Every drop of dew, a glimmering laugh,
Nature's own humor, a joyful path.

So dance with the leaves, let your heart play,
Join the merry chorus that brightens the day.
Under this sunlit, whimsical dome,
Every part of this world feels like home.

The Flow of Affection

In a river of giggles, we float along,
With ducks as our chorus, quacking a song.
The sun shines down with a wink so sly,
And clouds join in with their fluff from the sky.

A tree tells a riddle, its branches sway,
Leaves rustle laughter, come join in the fray.
Frogs leap in ponds, making splashes of glee,
Their tiny croaks echo like jubilee.

A picnic unfolds with sandwiches stacked,
While ants march in line, their tactics exact.
The lemonade sparkles, a bubbly parade,
In this bubbly world, laughter won't fade.

So splash in the puddles, let worries depart,
Join hands with the creatures, open your heart.
In this playful current of antics and cheer,
We'll surf on the waves, spreading joy, my dear!

A Tonic of Nostalgia

In a bottle of laughter, nostalgia sits,
With fizzy memories that never quit.
Old photos giggle, their edges all worn,
Recalling the days we all felt reborn.

The swing set creaks with a playful tone,
As whispers of mischief are cheerfully sown.
Kites dance in the breeze, painting the sky,
While candy wrappers tumble, time passing by.

Grandma's tales tickle in the evening glow,
In corners of kitchens where laughter can grow.
The smell of baked cookies swirls in the air,
Bringing sweet giggles that banish despair.

So raise a glass high to the moments we treasure,
Each sip of remembrance is purest of pleasure.
With every chuckle, a memory we find,
In our tonic of joy, we leave worries behind.

Arbor's Embrace

Beneath the vast branches, we gather with glee,
Where squirrels tell stories of mischief and spree.
The rhythm of rustling leaves keeps us warm,
While nature's embrace becomes our sweet charm.

In the shade of these giants, we tell silly tales,
Of giants and dragons and wind in our sails.
The bark cracks a smile, the roots root for fun,
All creatures join in, under the sun!

Picnic blankets spread, a feast quite absurd,
With sandwiches shaped like an oversized bird.
Laughter erupts with each silly bite,
In this woodland realm, everything's bright.

So let's twirl like leaves, let our spirits ascend,
Under this arbor, where joy has no end.
With every chuckle, the forest agrees,
Together forever, as playful as these!

Woodland Serenade

In the woods where squirrels prance,
Raccoons plot their secret dance.
A chipmunk shares a cheesy joke,
While crickets strum on sticks of oak.

The trees all giggle, leaves a-shake,
As mushrooms chuckle, for goodness sake!
A fox nearby rolls on the ground,
While owls hoot laughter all around.

A butterfly flutters, tickles my nose,
As bees buzz melodies that nobody knows.
Frogs croak tunes like a crazy band,
In this merry concert of the land.

Beneath bright blooms, with playful jest,
The woodland creatures are at their best.
Their laughter echoes, full of cheer,
In a wild serenade for all to hear.

Emotions in Bloom

In gardens lush where tickles grow,
The daisies wink, the sunflowers glow.
A rose declares with a silly pose,
I'm the best bloomer, just check my clothes!

Tulips trip on their fancy heels,
While violets giggle at their own appeals.
The lilies laugh with petals wide,
As buttercups join in for a ride.

Around the bees, a buzz of fun,
They dance through air, no worries, just run.
Oh, the scent of joy fills the air,
In this patch of happiness, we share.

A garden party, nature's delight,
With blossoms dancing into the night.
The laughter blossoms, bright and loud,
In a merry show, we are all proud.

A Potion of Fondness

In a cauldron bubbling, a secret mix,
With giggles of frogs and a sprinkle of tricks.
Toads leap in joy, they know it's grand,
While dandelions join in with a hand.

A dash of pine, a splash of glee,
Add some grasshoppers for a melody!
This potion of joy, it bubbles and steams,
Making laughter that's sweeter than dreams.

A pinch of thyme with a twist of lime,
The critters gather, it's potion time!
They sip and chuckle, the woodland cheers,
Laughter brewed through the years.

With every sip, the fun expands,
As they dance around in happy bands.
This brew of chuckles, it warms the heart,
In every critter's quirky part.

The Flowing Essence

A stream flows by with a giggling tune,
Where fish flip like they're on the moon.
A turtle paddles in a blurry whirl,
While frogs in silly breeches twirl.

The water sparkles, a shimmery grin,
As laughter flows, it's a splashy win.
A duck quacks jokes, with feathers bright,
Making waves of laughter take flight.

The rocks all chuckle, a playful crew,
They know just how to give a view.
Giggling minnows swim to and fro,
In the playful current of this funny flow.

Across the banks, the willows sway,
Joining in on this joyful play.
In this flowing essence of pure delight,
Nature's laughter shines, day and night.

Sweetness in the Veins

In the garden where laughter grows,
Sugar ants dance on their toes.
Puddles gleam in the summer glare,
Where giggles bubble, floating in the air.

A bee stings joy, but never despair,
Chasing dreams with a sticky flair.
Honey drips from the smile so wide,
As we skip along this sweet tide.

Each fruit a bauble, nature's jest,
Savoring life, we are truly blessed.
With every bite, we break into cheer,
Nothing's as sweet as good friends near.

Bouncing blooms and wobbly vines,
Laughter echoes, and brightly shines.
In this whimsical, juicy expanse,
We find silliness in every glance.

Heartstrings and Honey

A tale spun from laughter's thread,
With sticky notes on a blank head.
We pull the strings, they stretch and twang,
Oh, the silly, melodic clang!

A pot of gold, but filled with jam,
We toast to friendship—who gives a damn?
Each giggle bubbles like soda pop,
With every hiccup, we just can't stop.

Chasing quirks with a jolly breeze,
Tickling hearts with the greatest ease.
Winners we are in this fun race,
Not a single sour face.

Our words whirl like a candy whirl,
In this grove, our hearts unfurl.
With honeyed memories on the fly,
Let's dance to life, just you and I.

The Elixir of Remembrance

A potion brewed with laughter's grace,
Each swirl a smile, a knowing face.
We sip the memories, sweet and bright,
Turning mundane into pure delight.

Time tickles as we clink our cups,
Sharing tales of hiccups and hiccups.
A wink, a nudge, stories unfold,
In this brew, friendship is gold.

Elixirs burst with comic fare,
As giggles rise without a care.
Each drop a memory, a gentle tease,
In this bizarre, syrupy breeze.

We churn the past with playful zest,
Never knowing which jest is best.
Let's toast to chuckles, the heart's embrace,
In a whirlwind of joy, our sacred space.

Tendrils of Connection

Weaving tales with vines so green,
Roots entwined in the best scene.
A ticklish breeze along the path,
Turning giggles into a hearty laugh.

With every hug, our branches sway,
Growing closer with each silly play.
Our hearts connected, a quirky blend,
In this garden, joy won't end.

Silly moments, like flowers sprout,
Petals giggle, there's no doubt.
Searching for sunshine, we mimic the bees,
Buzzing with laughter in the trees.

While roots dig deep into fun soil,
We cultivate grown-ups who can toil.
In this tangled web of quirky fate,
Life's laughter beckons, let's celebrate!

Heartwood Harmonies

In the trunk where laughter grows,
A squirrel's dance in leafy shows,
Nutty jokes and chubby sprites,
All gather round for silly nights.

Beneath the bark, a melody,
Jokes and giggles stuck like honey,
Whispers of woodpeckers so bright,
Tickle the heart in pure delight.

Branches sway with tales so bold,
Saw that tree do something told,
When clouds burst into laughter's cheer,
Nature's punchline draws us near.

Roots are tickling in the ground,
They're having parties, gathering round,
With worms that wiggle, sing a tune,
While stars above wink at the moon.

The Aroma of Aged Memories.

In the cellar, old bottles grinned,
Whispers of wine where fun began,
Corked secrets bubble up with glee,
Oh, the stories stuck in memory!

Barrels full of laughter stew,
Each sip brings a chuckle or two,
Grapes on vines spinning tales so fine,
Pour me a glass, it's giggle time!

Dusty corners with ghosts of cheer,
Faded jokes linger, crystal clear,
A toast to moments, a wink, a cheer,
Aged to perfection, we hold them dear.

As the cork pops with a playful sound,
Joy releases, swirling all around,
With every swig, we dance and sway,
Turning time's laughter into play.

Nature's Whisper

Rustling leaves in the morning light,
Breeze telling jokes, what a delight!
Bees buzz around, performing a show,
With petals dancing, stealing the flow.

Clouds roll in with a fluffy grin,
Tickling the skies, let the fun begin!
Raindrops laugh as they patter down,
Kicking up puddles in the town.

Squirrels trade nuts like toasty notes,
While frogs croak punchlines that tickle our throats,
Each corner of green sings silly rhymes,
Nature's the bard, making merry times.

So when the dawn calls us awake,
Join the laughter, for laughter's sake,
In the wild where whimsy grows,
The sweetest giggles find us close.

The Heart's Resin

In the woods where giggles freeze,
The trees stick together like old friends,
Resin drips with a playful shout,
Sticky secrets trapped all about.

Pine cones drop with a thud and bounce,
Filling the air with a joking flounce,
Nature's glue in a crafty plot,
Holds memories in every knot.

Branches peek with an eager glance,
Inviting critters to join the dance,
The woodland floor, a stage so grand,
With tiny feet lending a hand.

So come and smell the joyous pine,
A whiff of laughter, oh how divine!
In every tear that the trees confess,
Life's funny moments we must dress.

Vitality of the Heart

In a garden where laughter blooms,
The flowers wear their funny costumes.
Bees buzz jokes, oh what a sound,
Tickling petals, joy all around.

The sun winks bright, a cheeky flare,
As daisies dance without a care.
Grass blades hum a silly tune,
Under the gaze of a grinning moon.

Each raindrop falls with a playful plop,
You can hear the teapots laugh and hop.
Nature's giggles, a sweet delight,
Everything's funny in the morning light.

And when the day gives way to night,
Stars join in, twinkling so bright.
With every chuckle from the trees,
Love's a joke that brings you to your knees.

An Essence to Remember

A whiff of humor fills the air,
A fragrant blend beyond compare.
Petunias wear a silly hat,
As squirrels steal snacks, imagine that!

The breeze carries laughter on its wings,
While crickets chirp the joy it brings.
Butterflies giggle in the sun's warm glow,
As shadows play tag; oh, what a show!

A sunflower tells a joke so tall,
And with that giggle, petals fall.
Even the roses can't help but snicker,
At tulips prancing, getting quicker!

In this garden of mirth and cheer,
Every moment brings us near.
So twirl in laughter, don't just remember,
The essence of joy is a sweet, warm ember.

Liquid Whispers

Raindrops dance on a windowpane,
Whispers of joy, oh what a rain!
Every droplet tells a tale,
Of mischievous cats and a squirrel's wail.

A puddle laughs, splashing around,
While umbrellas frown, upside-down.
Each ripple sings in its own tune,
As rubber ducks float, oh how they swoon!

A stream of giggles flows so free,
With fish that wink, as if to tease.
The alligators grin wide and bright,
Making silly faces with all their might!

So catch your breath amidst the fun,
As watercolors splash and run.
In this world of giggles and glee,
Life's liquid whispers aren't just for me!

Shades of Affection

Colors swirl in a playful fight,
Like crayons mixing, pure delight.
A warm orange blush, a greenish tease,
They share a wink with the gentle breeze.

In a canvas of chuckles and beams,
Love is splashed in the wildest dreams.
Each shade a memory, bright and clear,
Painting smiles that draw us near.

A splash of blue for the laughter shared,
While a blush of pink shows how we cared.
Purple giggles stretch out wide,
As laughter dances on love's soft tide.

So let your heart be a palette bright,
Layered in shades of pure delight.
With every stroke on this canvas we paint,
The colors of joy are never faint.

Earth's Tender Touch

Beneath the tree, a squirrel dreams,
A nut in hand, or so it seems.
A playful dance, a cartwheel spun,
He slips and slides, oh what a fun!

The grass beneath his tiny paws,
A ticklish prank with nature's laws.
He laughs aloud, the leaves all cheer,
A woodland party, oh so near!

With twigs as hats and acorns fine,
The forest friends all sip on pine.
Their giggles rise like morning dew,
In this wild world, joy's never through.

So next you walk beneath a bough,
Remember this, oh, come and vow.
Life's quirky moments, soft and sweet,
Are sprinkled here at nature's feet.

The Vitality of Emotion

A porcupine that's feeling shy,
Waves his quills, oh my, oh my!
He pricks a friend, then laughs with glee,
"Just testing friendship, can't you see?"

A chipmunk giggles, "Oh, be still!
Your social game could use some skill."
They share a laugh, forget the prick,
A bond so tight, it's quite the trick!

In the jungle, monkeys swing,
Chasing after joy, that's their thing.
They throw a fruit, a sly old jest,
The funniest games put hearts to test.

Emotions flutter like a breeze,
In every laugh, with joy we seize.
So let the quirks of life unroll,
Laughter keeps the heart so whole.

Flowing through Memories

A river's flow whispers tales of old,
Where fish wear hats, if truth be told.
They swim and splash, with glee abound,
In bubbles of laughter, secrets found.

A turtle in glasses reads the news,
"Water's rising, but I refuse!"
He sips his tea, a bit too slow,
But memories of youth make rivers flow.

A frog croaks jokes, the crowd erupts,
His puns so silly, the laughter cups.
With every leap, he tells a tale,
Of love and joy that'll never pale.

So as you stroll along that stream,
Hear the whispers, feel the dream.
Memories flow, like water free,
Bring laughter home, just wait and see.

The Confluence of Feelings

In a meadow bright, emotions gleam,
Butterflies waltz, like a sweet dream.
One flaps too hard and collides with a bee,
"Hey, watch it!" buzzes, "You startled me!"

A rabbit hops, with joy on its face,
"A dance-off here, it's a happy place!"
They leap and twirl, oh what a sight,
In a conga line, from day till night.

The daisies sway, with laughter they hum,
A squirrel joins in, look how he runs!
Their giggles rise with the evening sun,
In this garden of glee, no one's outdone.

So gather round, let's share a smile,
In nature's heart, let's pause awhile.
For feelings mingle, just let them be,
In this swirl of joy, you'll find the key!

The Bonding Essence

In the kitchen, chaos reigns always,
Spaghetti flies in a dance of craze.
Tomato sauce splatters like abstract art,
Yet laughter stitches the mess apart.

The dog sneezes, the cat makes a leap,
While grandma's cookies just can't help but beep.
Family hugs in a mishmash of glee,
Basil's whispering, 'This is pure comedy!'

A flour fight breaks out, joy fills the air,
Ladies giggle, while men just stand and stare.
The carrot dodges a flying potato,
Dinner's a circus, zero chance of a fiasco.

As we gather, we blend in silly ways,
Each moment a color, brightening our days.
With jokes as our glue, we stick and we sway,
In this charming mess, we find our play.

Echoes of the Forest

Trees stand tall, but squirrels play tricks,
They hide acorns just for cheap kicks.
Branches giggle, leaves dance around,
Nature's whispers create a blend profound.

Beneath the canopy, shadows grow wide,
Mushrooms don hats, while chipmunks collide.
A raccoon steals snacks, oh what a sight,
In this wild laughter, everything feels right.

Frogs croak jokes from the murky deep,
While owls hoot riddles that make us leap.
Each gust of wind carries quirky delight,
As woodland confetti bursts into light.

Together we wander, through giggles and snorts,
Finding joy in the quiet, with woodland cavorts.
In echoes of laughter, we joyfully blend,
A memory forged, where nature won't end.

Fleeting Drizzle

A sudden shower, umbrellas on the run,
Splashing puddles, oh what fun!
Raindrops dance on pavement's stage,
Each drop a performer, engaging the age.

Giggling children lose their sleek shoes,
As laughter mingles with the wet blues.
Watercolors paint our cheeky grins,
While in this moment, joyous chaos begins.

Lightning flashes, and we all scream,
Spinning in the rain like a silly dream.
Thunder's a drummer, keeping the beat,
With nature's rhythm, we shuffle our feet.

As the clouds smile down, we chase the breeze,
In fleeting droplets, we find our ease.
With humor as raindrops, we splash and tease,
This whimsical moment, a joyful masterpiece.

The Tapestry of Feelings

At a party with friends, the vibe is so bright,
Each joke a stitch, holding us tight.
Punch flows freely, spills on the floor,
Yet smiles are woven, always wanting more.

A mishmash of stories, each one absurd,
From groans and guffaws, our voices are heard.
Unexpected hugs, the dance of delight,
In this patchwork of joy, we party all night.

With clumsy twirls, we trip over glee,
Emotions a quilt, as silly as can be.
Socks with polka dots, and ties that don't match,
In this colorful chaos, we blissfully catch.

Though life may tangle like yarn in the fray,
With laughter as thread, we create our bouquet.
Feelings entwined, like vines in bright bloom,
In this tapestry woven, we banish the gloom.

Softness in the Breeze

A gentle breeze whispers near,
It swirls and twirls without fear.
It tickles my nose and makes me sneeze,
Oh, the joys of dancing leaves with ease.

A tumbleweed rolls, a sight so sly,
It's got more moves than I can try.
Each flurry gives my thoughts a spin,
Nature's giggle draws us all in.

Laughter flows in playful sighs,
As clouds form funny, silly guise.
The sun winks down, a cheeky chap,
Chasing shadows that start to nap.

So let the soft breeze frolic and play,
Bringing smiles to brighten the day.
With every gust, let charm unleash,
In this fluffy world, we find our peace.

The Essence of Echoes

In the valley of chuckles, echoes sing,
Twisting and turning, just like spring.
A voice calls out, and I reprise,
Like a parrot with untrained eyes.

The hills are tired of my ancient joke,
But they can't escape, no matter how they poke.
Each rib-tickler bounces back in glee,
A rumor of giggles floats carelessly.

With every shout, the valleys roar,
As nature's laughter unlocks the door.
It spreads like butter on warm toast,
In this echo chamber, I'll gladly boast.

So let's gather round this sound parade,
Where laughter's echo will never fade.
The essence of joy, we'll gladly bless,
In this echoing world of silliness.

Glistening Hearts

In the garden of giggles, happiness blooms,
With glistening hearts that chase the gloom.
One poppy sways with a wink in its eye,
As bees dance in circles, oh my, oh my!

A sunflower chuckles with golden rays,
Waving to daisies in bright, silly ways.
The petals tickle, a vibrant spree,
In this patch of joy, we're all so free.

The blooms unite in a colorful show,
Dressed to impress in a vibrant flow.
Each spark of laughter, a fragrant delight,
With glistening hearts, we soar like a kite.

So let's gather petals and share the cheer,
With glistening hearts, there's nothing to fear.
In this garden of fun, we'll plant our seeds,
And watch them grow into heartfelt deeds.

Syrupy Reveries

A drizzle of sweetness upon my tongue,
With each sticky sip, I'm forever young.
Like a pancake party that's never done,
These syrupy dreams are pure, sticky fun!

I spill a bit here, I spill a bit there,
This gooey concoction is beyond compare.
With laughter that bubbles and hearts that sing,
This sweet surprise falls under the fling.

Pour it on waffles, let's stack them high,
A syrupy tower that'll touch the sky.
Each drop a giggle, each glop a cheer,
In this sweetened world, we have nothing to fear.

So let's embrace this sugary dream,
Where memories stick and laughter streams.
With syrupy reveries that shine so bright,
We'll tap dance together through the night.

Tides of Tenderness

In a patch of clover, a bumblebee buzzed,
Sipping on flowers, all sticky and fuzzed.
He met a shy snail, who slipped out for a chat,
"Your shell's quite a burden!" said the bee to the rat.

They chuckled and giggled, oh what a delight,
Sharing their secrets in the warm evening light.
"Let's race to the daisies!" the bee took a chance,
With a whir and a whirl, they twirled in a dance.

Under the moonlight, the tasks seem so grand,
The snail boasts of journeys across the whole sand.
"You're quick as a flash!" said the snail with a grin,
While the bee, slightly dizzy, just swayed in a spin.

Together they laughed as they crawled and they flew,
Finding joy in the little things, simple and true.
A friendship so quirky, it grew every day,
Two unlikely buddies, come what may.

Tree-Born Murmurs

In a forest so vibrant, the branches do sway,
A squirrel and a crow plan mischief today.
"Let's take all the acorns and stash them away!"
Said the crow with a caw, feeling clever and fey.

But the squirrel just chuckled, with a twitch of his tail,
"You'll never beat me! I'm the acorn detail!"
So they plotted and laughed, both quick on their feet,
In a wild race for treasure, who would take the sweet?

The crow flew above, flapping loud like a drum,
While the squirrel dashed down, oh so fast, here he'd come!
"You can have the left side; I'll stick to the right!"
"But your side's all the juicy ones, what a sight!"

The branches were shaking with giggles galore,
As they stumbled through laughter, then fell to the floor.
The trees whispered softly, "Now isn't this fun?"
A frolic of beings sharing laughs 'til they're done.

Elixirs of Emotion

In a patchwork of blooms, two bees in a fight,
Over petals and nectar, it's quite a delight.
One said, "My honey's the best, can't you see?"
The other buzzed back, "Well, mine's sweeter, let's be!"

They argued and haggled, what a comical scene,
While the flowers just nodded, and giggled between.
"Let's blend our wild tastes! Create a new mix!"
They shared their concoctions, with flicks and with tricks.

"This blend tastes like sunshine!" the first one exclaimed,
While the other just laughed, sweet nectar had claimed.
They clinked tiny wings, what a marvelous find,
Cooperation and sweetness, all in the mind.

With each sticky sip, more ideas took flight,
As they created a brew that was sheer pure delight.
The hive rumbled laughter, what a buzz on the wing,
Turns out blending flavors makes the heart happy sing.

The Pulse of the Forest

In a tangled thicket, a frog on a log,
Croaked out a riddle, confused a young dog.
"Why do you jump?" the pup tilted his head,
"To catch all the flies, now that's what I said!"

The dog chuckled loudly, "You jump way too high!"
And the frog just replied, with a wink of his eye.
"Life's a great leap, my fluffy-tailed friend,
So come join the frolic, there's fun without end!"

On a meadow of daisies, they played all the day,
Learning new tricks in a hops-and-wags way.
The squirrels rolled over, they howled from the trees,
"Those two make a riot! What a sight, oh, please!"

As the sunset painted hues, all pinks and of gold,
The forest breathed deep, in the stories retold.
A friendship so silly, not bound by any aim,
Just two joyful hearts, forever in the game.

Mellow Encounters

In the garden, bees do dance,
A flower's scent, a silly chance.
We chuckle at the buzzing crew,
While sipping teas, just me and you.

Lemonade spills down my chin,
A sticky mess, but we both grin.
You toss a berry, oh what fun!
We laugh until the day is done.

A squirrel steals my snack away,
I shout, "Hey! Come back and play!"
You laugh so hard, I start to tear,
Those furry thieves, they bring good cheer.

Together in this sunny space,
With wild jokes, we fill the place.
Life's sweetest moments, never planned,
In goofy joy, we both will stand.

The Brew of Memories

Coffee beans in bacon pants,
A brewing storm of coffee dance.
You spill the cream, I make a scene,
We laugh so hard, it's quite obscene.

Your hat is tipped, what a sight,
As coffee hops and takes a flight.
We giggle as the dog joins in,
With slurps and snorts, we can't begin.

Each sip a memory, bold and bright,
The flavor mixed with pure delight.
Today's disaster, now a song,
In every drop, we can't go wrong.

With sugar plumes and laughter swirls,
We share our tales like silly girls.
A mug of dreams, a dash of cheer,
With every sip, our hearts draw near.

The Taste of Reminiscence

Tasting sweets from days gone by,
A cherry pie makes me sigh.
You trip and fall on whipped cream glaze,
We roll on floors in laughter's blaze.

Candies stuck in every shoe,
Old memories, the tales they brew.
A cupcake fight, oh what a blast,
Sprinkles flying, memories cast.

Your nose is pink with frosting charm,
I shove a pie, no cause for alarm.
Together we create a mess,
But in this chaos, we feel blessed.

With cookie crumbs and juice that stains,
We dance around in sweet refrains.
Each laugh a morsel, joy our feast,
The silly moments never ceased.

Words Woven in Nature

In whispered winds and rustling leaves,
We weave our tales, nature believes.
A silly tale of a frog in shoes,
Croaking rhymes, we can't refuse.

Underneath the blooming tree,
You trip on roots, oh can't you see?
Your laugh rings out, a melody,
With every twist, pure harmony.

The clouds will giggle, they pass on by,
While silly birds sing sweet and spry.
In every rustle, a joke will land,
As nature weaves our lives so grand.

With every branch that bows and creaks,
Our banter flows, the fun it peaks.
In the quiet woods, we find our voice,
And in each chuckle, we rejoice.

Sweets of the Heart

Chocolate drips from cheek to chin,
Laughter erupts with every grin.
Candy-coated jokes take flight,
Sugar highs keep hearts so light.

Marshmallow hugs and gummy bear cheer,
Sweetness lingers, always near.
Lollipop dreams and taffy pulls,
Life is better with candy rules.

Sticky hands and silly fights,
Popcorn kernels on laughter nights.
Giggles stuck like bubblegum,
In this sweetness, we're never glum.

A sugary dance around the floor,
With every step, we laugh some more.
So let's embrace this moment sweet,
As heart-shaped treats, we're hard to beat.

The Flowing Heartstream

My heart's a river, flowing wide,
With silly fish that dance inside.
They twirl and swirl with goofy glee,
Making waves just to tease me!

The current's strong with chuckles bright,
As rubber ducks take their flight.
Floating by with giggles near,
Their silly quacks, all I can hear!

A waterfall of laughter spills,
With splashes that ignite the thrills.
Canoes of joy, they paddle fast,
In this stream, we're free at last!

So dip your toes and take a plunge,
In this laughter, let's all lunge.
Our hearts adrift on this fine stream,
With silly fish in a joyful theme!

Harmonies of Nature

A bird sings out a tuneful laugh,
While trees do sway, a leafy staff.
The flowers giggle, petals sway,
In the garden of joy, we play.

Bees buzz by with silly plans,
Dancing in their tiny bands.
Ladybugs wear polka-dot pride,
As the sunbeams act as our guide.

Rivers chuckle with every flow,
While the winds join in the show.
Behold the blooms that wink and cheer,
Nature's giggles, loud and clear!

Under the sky, we twirl and sing,
In this laughter, we find our spring.
A harmony of nature's art,
Together, we share this joyful heart!

A Dance of Affection

In the ballroom of bizarre delight,
We prance around, oh what a sight!
With two left feet, we trip and twirl,
In this dance, let laughter swirl.

The music plays a jolly tune,
As we laugh beneath the moon.
With each misstep, our hearts take flight,
In this fun, we feel just right.

A tango of mishaps and silly spins,
Together, we lose and then we wins.
With every fall, we just can't pout,
In this dance, it's joy, no doubt!

So raise a toast with fizzy cheer,
To wild steps and friends so dear.
In this dance, let's jump and sway,
With a giggle, we'll play all day!

Sweet Serendipity

In the garden where laughter blooms,
A squirrel dances, chasing brooms.
Honey drips from a bee's tiny cap,
While clumsy kids perform a lap.

Butterflies twirl in fancy gowns,
Tickling noses of sleepy hounds.
The sun giggles, playing peek-a-boo,
As shadows stretch, joining the view.

Jellybeans jump, quite out of line,
A parade of flavors, oh so fine!
Lemon drops slip, causing a fall,
While licorice laughs, immune to it all.

Under the sky, like a whipped cream pie,
Surprises come like a baking high.
Chirps and chirrups create a tune,
In this carnival, where chaos is swoon.

A Tidal Wave of Feelings

Waves crash down, like clumsy hugs,
Seagulls squawk, in morning mugs.
Sand tickles toes, a slippery dance,
While jellyfish float in childish prance.

Sunshine drizzles, melting hearts,
As beach balls sail in playful arts.
Crabs put on their finest pinches,
While laughter bubbles, no room for winces.

Kites snag trees, like tousled hair,
And giggles escape, filling the air.
Footprints marvelous, in twisting roads,
Followed by laughter, as joy explodes.

Under the sun, mischief abounds,
In this ocean of playful sounds.
With each splash, emotions inflate,
Forget the clock, levitate, celebrate!

Harmony in the Air

A pigeon struts in snazzy shoes,
While a mouse dons a floral snooze.
Balancing dreams on the wind's bright back,
Chasing giggles, in a comic flack.

Clouds fluff up, like popcorn balls,
Rain drops dance, a chorus calls.
Bees join in with their buzzing cheer,
As flowers wiggle, drawing near.

The sun rolls in with a chuckle deep,
Kicking shadows, that try to creep.
Ducks don sunglasses, croon a song,
In this mixed-up world, where all belong.

Mirth is woven in the fragrant breeze,
As whispers tickle like falling leaves.
Harmony sings on this carefree ride,
A merry garden of joy and pride.

Silhouettes of Emotion

In twilight shadows, giggles flare,
Cats tiptoe through a dance of air.
Balloons bounce in the fading light,
While roosters croon their sleepy delight.

Chairs wobble and planks go squeak,
As mischief's essence makes us weak.
Jump ropes hum with a playful twist,
While moonbeams play a misfit list.

Sneezes echo, like softest bells,
As laughter tumbles in joyful swells.
Fireflies blink in synchrony bright,
Creating a scene, pure and light.

In a cactus patch, laughter's a bloom,
Tickling toes in nature's room.
Silhouettes dance, as day bids goodbye,
In this funny world, we'll always fly.

www.ingramcontent.com/pod-product-compliance
Lightning Source LLC
Chambersburg PA
CBHW051645160426
43209CB00004B/798